I0837419

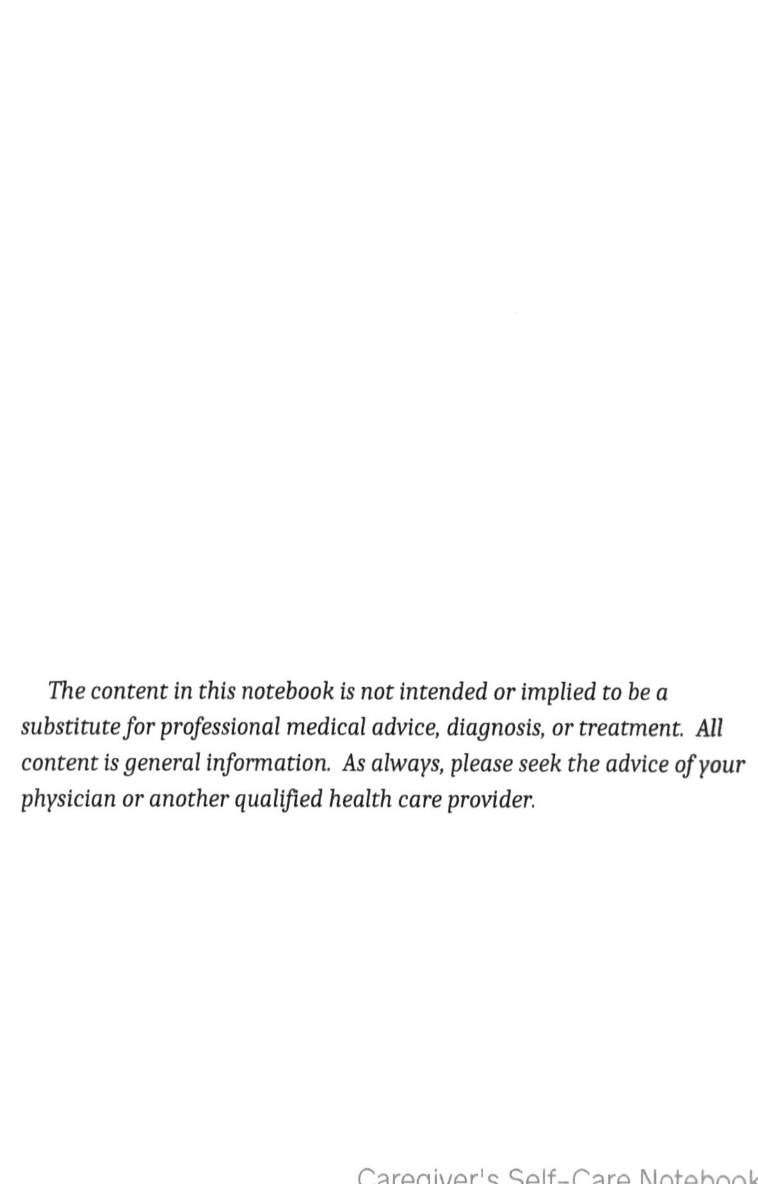

Caregiver's Self-Care Notebook

Self-Care

Maintaining and improving all aspects of one's health and well being. Any practice completed or avoided in an effort to take care of one's self.

-- Take Care

This Notebook is
Dedicated To

Above all else, guard your heart, for everything you do flows from it. -Proverbs 4:23 NIV

This notebook was designed for caregivers from all walks of life...

- **Guardians** taking care of their special needs children & elderly parents.

- **People** looking after sick spouses and loved ones.

- **Nurses** and **healthcare professionals** in homes & hospitals.

- **Nannies, au pairs, babysitters, watchful neighbors, volunteers,** and **anyone** who cares for others.

The ability to care for others is a blessing, but that does not mean it is easy.

From nurses who care for people for a living, to families & friends who do so out of love--caregivers know that taking care of other people is a tremendous undertaking that requires compassion, time, and skill.

 The duties of a caregiver are never-ending. It is important to mind all aspects of your own health so that you can show up as your best self.

Why is "Self-Care for Caregivers" so important?

Anyone who provides care for another person is at risk for burn-out.

Caregiver's Self-Care Notebook

Small amounts of stress are normal and necessary for our well-being, but chronic stress can be very damaging to the body.

Chronic stress can lead to a myriad of preventable, mental, emotional, and physical health problems.

It's impossible to do away with all sources of stress, but managing your emotions and developing an effective stress management plan can help.

Practicing self care can be compared to the 'Oxygen Mask' principle. In case of emergency on an airplane, it is always advised to apply your own mask before attempting to help other passengers with their masks.

   The theory is quite simple--a person who depletes all of their energy administering oxygen to others, might not have the energy to save their own life.

This concept is applicable in all aspects of life, including caregiving. You have to take care of yourself first, or you will be no good to the people that you support.

Poor self care practices can lead to a serious decline in personal health status.

Pause to Practice Self-Care

- **Pause** -Stay encouraged.

- **Use your resources** -Be open to accepting help from family members. Look into respite care, cleaning, and meal preparation services.

- **Prioritize Health** -Make and keep all health-related appointments, including preventative, routine exams, and problem visits.

- **Plan** -If you can make things easier for yourself, do it. Plan, plan, plan! Meals, workouts, care, routines, and breaks. Write down ways to make things easier for yourself.

- **ME Time** -Remember to take care of yourself. If your mind and body are not working, you are no good to anyone else.

- **Be Positive** -Maintain a positive attitude. Not only will you feel better, but your positive energy will rub off on the person for which you are providing care.

Consider These Resources for Caregivers

- Caregiver Support Groups
- Mental Health Counseling
- Religious Support Groups
- Disease/Diagnosis Specific Support Groups

- Additional Resources
  -https://www.hhs.gov/programs/providers-and-facilities/resources-for-caregivers/index.html

  -U.S. Department of Veteran's Affairs Caregiver Support: 1-855-260-3274

  -http://www.caregiveraction.org
  -https://www.caregiving.org

Stress does not have a uniform presentation.

Stress can manifest in different ways, in different people.

Signs of Stress

- Avoiding other responsibilities

- Short-tempered, irritable

- Feelings of hopelessness, guilt, or isolation

- Depression, disturbances in sleep hygiene

- GI distress, change in eating habits

- Chronic fatigue

- Muscle tension or pain

- General malaise or weakness

- Headaches

- Sweating, rash, or other skin issues

- Rapid breathing or heart rate

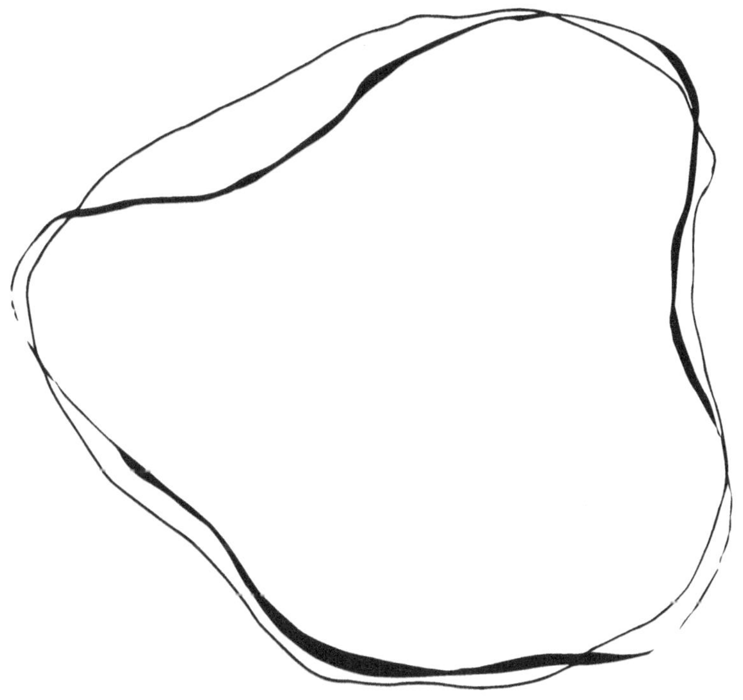

<u>Signs That I'm Stressed:</u>

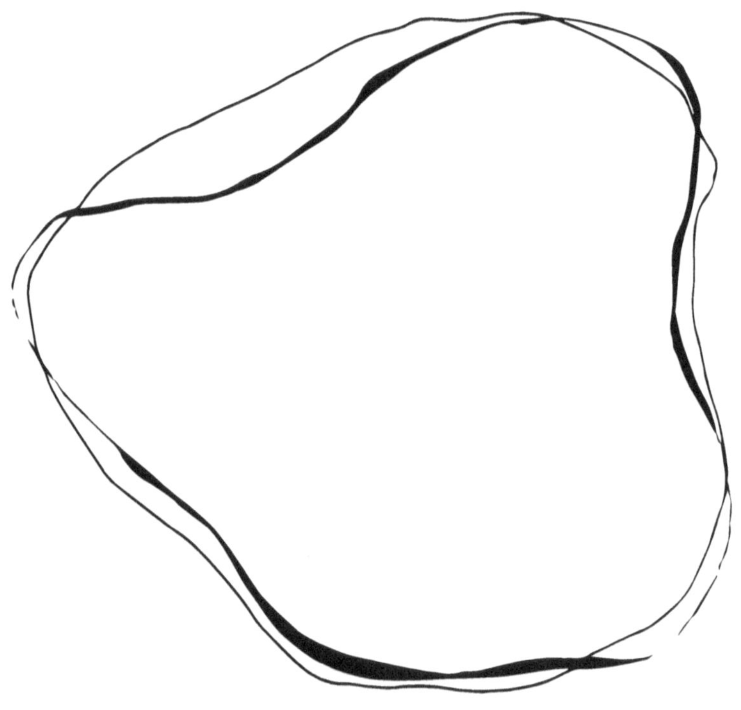

Stress Management Plan

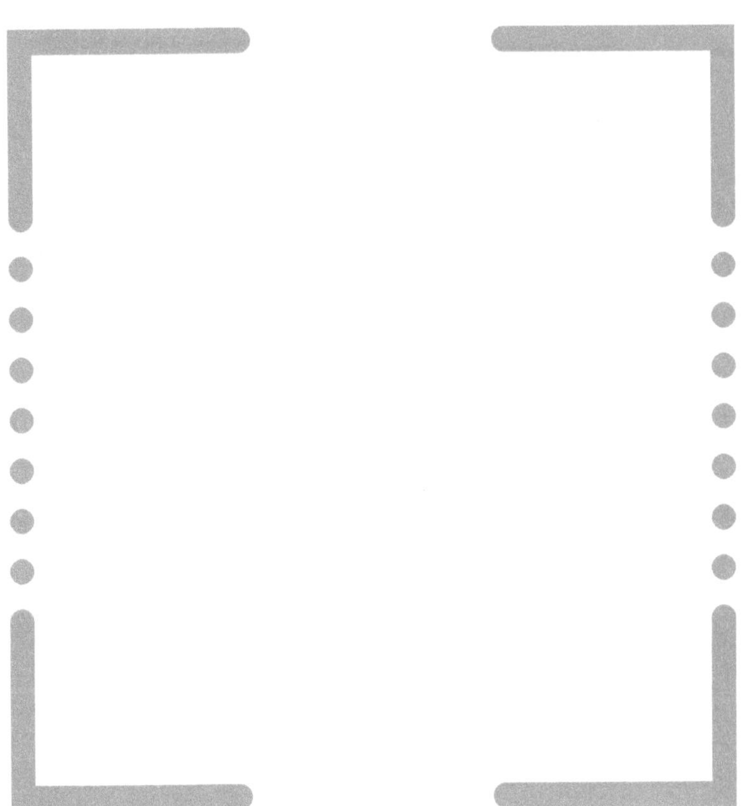

Stress Management Plan

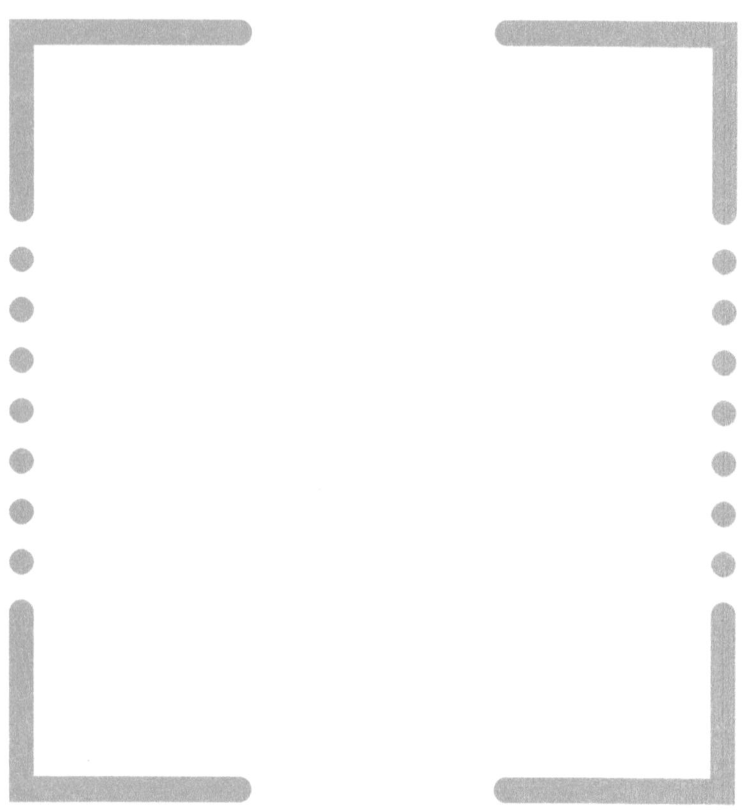

As busy caregivers, it is not always possible to carve out extended blocks of time for rest and reflection. Make the most out of even the smallest breaks.

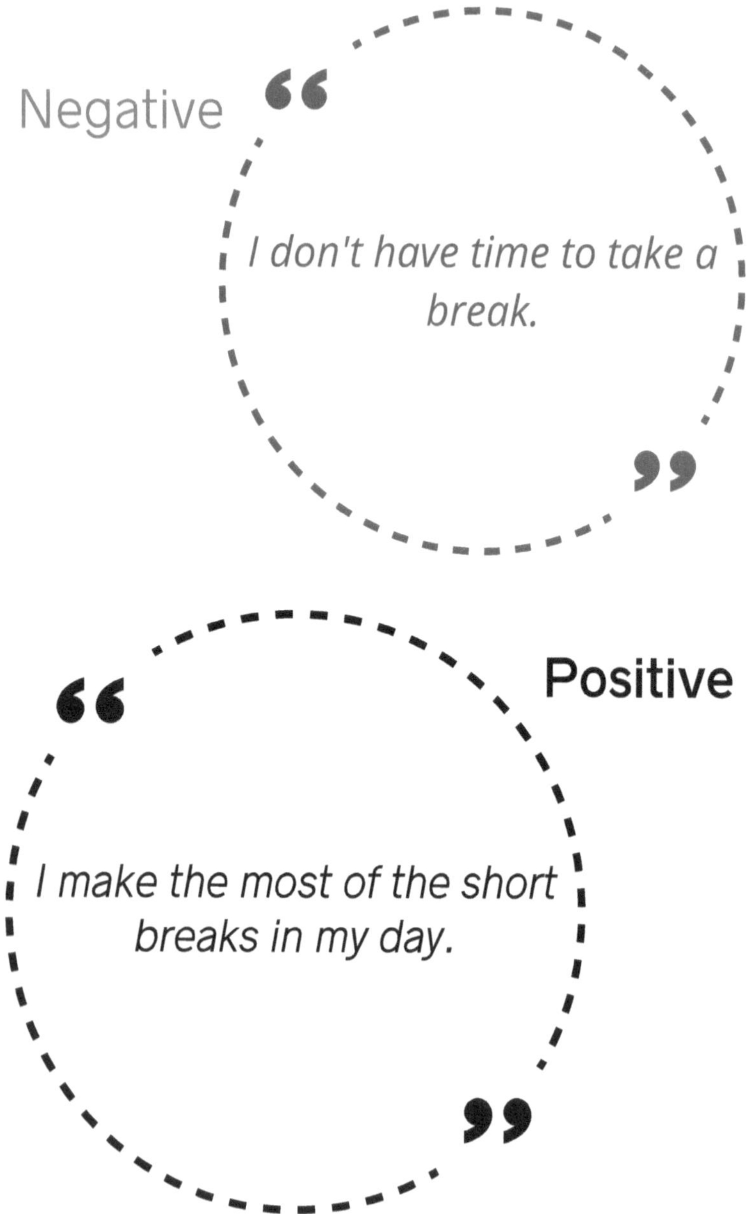

Negative
I don't have time to take a break.
Positive
I make the most of the short breaks in my day.

And he said to them, "Come away by yourselves to a desolate place and rest a while." For many were coming and going, and they had no leisure even to eat. -Mark 6:31 ESV

Quick Ways to Pause & Reset

- Change your environment

- Take a bathroom break

- Make/listen to a music or podcast playlist

- Read or listen to a book

- Pray

- Breathe

- Meditate

Quick Ways to Pause & Reset

- Step outside to connect with nature

- Phone a friend

- Stretch

- Sit in your car

- Write or draw

- Grab a snack

- Take a shower, bath, or nap

How Can I Make the **Most** of My Breaks?

Caregiver's Self-Care Notebook

How Can I Make the **Most** of My Breaks?

Caregiver's Self-Care Notebook

Pause to Meditate

Benefits of Meditation

- Improved sleep and focus

- Enhanced mood & emotional stability

- Reduced anxiety, blood pressure, & inflammation

- Increased energy, self-control & self-management skills

- Encourages complete oxygen exchange

- Easy, no equipment needed, accessible anywhere

> To meditate means to go home to yourself. Then you know how to take care of the things that are happening inside you, and how to take care of the things that happen around you.

-Thich Nhat Hanh

Meditation
Points to Remember

- <u>Focus. on. each. breath.</u>

- Return to the present if your mind wanders.

- Pay attention to your body. Notice areas of tension and attempt to relax & release.

- Express gratitude.

- Give yourself grace. Your meditation practice can be anything that you want it to be.

Caregiver's Self-Care Notebook

Caregiver's Self-Care Notebook

Pause to
Breathe

Caregiver's Self-Care Notebook

Pause to
Breathe

"Breathe. Let go. And remind yourself that this very moment is the only one you know you have for sure."

OPRAH WINFREY

Pause to Reflect

Caregiver's Self-Care Notebook

Pause to Reflect

Pause to Reflect

Caregiver's Self-Care Notebook

Pause to Reflect

Pause to Reflect

Pause to Check
Your Energy

Energy

Energy transfers really do exist. If you've ever interacted with a 'Negative Nelly' co-worker or family member, you understand this concept. These people are widely known as 'energy vampires' because they can literally drain your energy if you are not careful.

As caregivers, our energy can move on to our loved ones and patients, even when we do not realize it.

Working with children with special needs for years has given me first-hand experience with the principle of energetic exchanges. For example, if I started the shift with a positive attitude, the children's emotions would soon follow suit. On the other hand, if I unknowingly brought in negative energy due to exhaustion or a challenging time prior to work, the children's energy also reflected mine.

Energy

If we fix our energy, we can fix our lives. Create the most positive mindset--not only when caring for others, but also during interactions with self. Use positive, reassuring language during self-talk. Be mindful of your energy exchanges.

Energy

Humans can transfer energies to each other and they can connect with nature's healing energy. Walking outside barefoot is only one connecting/grounding technique that decrease anxiety and stress. Some studies suggest that grounding can have positive health benefits at the cellular level.

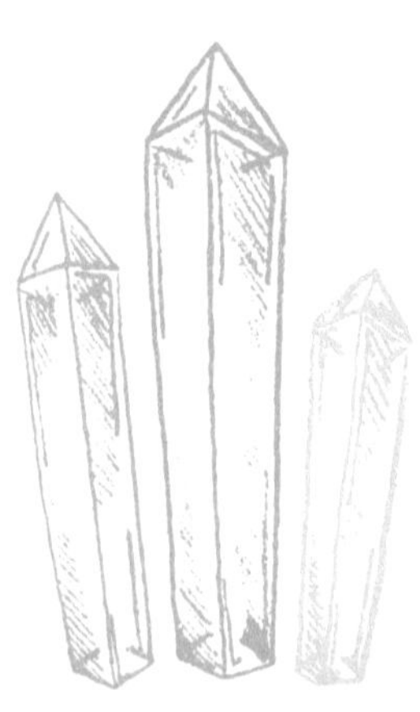

Tips on Grounding/Reconnecting with Nature

- Focus on your sense of touch

- Make contact with different aspects of nature (water, sun, trees, the ground)

- Practice deep breathing

- Stretch or engage in movement

- Listen to the sounds in your environment

- Notice your body cues and positioning

- Inhale your atmosphere

Grounding/Mindfulness Exercise

- FIVE things you can SEE [Notice the details, colors, etc.]

- FOUR things you can FEEL [Notice the temperature & texture.]

- THREE things you can HEAR [Notice the tone and quality of voices, pitch of nature's sounds, etc.]

- TWO things you can SMELL [Notice the characteristics of the scents around you.]

- ONE thing you can TASTE.

Energy Affirmations

I can do all things through Christ which strengthens me.

I release all things that are not meant for me.

I create the life that I want to live.

I cast my cares on The Lord.

I do not worry.

I start fresh when I need to.

I welcome blessings and positivity into my life.

I am making new habits.

I set my own boundaries.

I am safe from all harm.

I breathe in the positive, and release the negative.

Affirmations for Positive Energy

Positive Energy Affirmations

Caregiver's Self-Care Notebook

Positive Energy Affirmations

Caregiver's Self-Care Notebook

Pause & Raise Your Vibration

- Start and maintain routines

- Practice gratitude regularly

- Eat a balanced diet

- Set boundaries

- Cultivate your support system

- Limit time on devices

- Drink water and stay hydrated

- Smudge (sage) your space

- Do something kind for someone else

Energy Check

Energy is contagious:
either you affect people
or infect people.

Pause to Pray

Whoever dwells in the shelter
of the Most High will rest in
the shadow of the almighty.
-Psalm 91 NIV

Pause to Pray

Caregiver's Self-Care Notebook

Pause to Pray

Caregiver's Self-Care Notebook

Pause to Pray

Caregiver's Self-Care Notebook

Pause to Pray

Caregiver's Self-Care Notebook

"PRAYER IS SIMPLY TALKING TO GOD LIKE A FRIEND AND SHOULD BE THE EASIEST THING WE DO EACH DAY."

-Joyce Meyer

Pause to Set-Goals

Caregiver's Self-Care Notebook

Pause to Set-Goals

Caregiver's Self-Care Notebook

Pause to Set-Goals

Pause to Set-Goals

Caregiver's Self-Care Notebook

Pause to Set-Goals

Pause to Plan

Caregiver's Self-Care Notebook

Pause to Plan

Caregiver's Self-Care Notebook

My Plans for Success

What changes can I implement to make life easier?

My Plans for Success

What changes can I implement to make life easier?

My Plans for Success

What changes can I implement to make life easier?

What changes can I implement to make life easier?

My Plans for Success

What changes can I implement to make life easier?

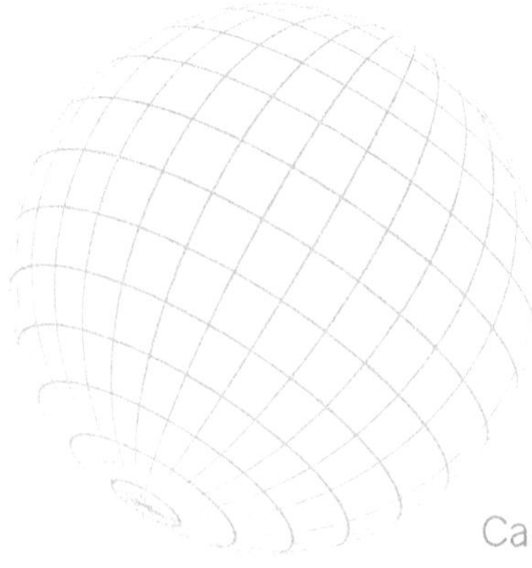

My Plans for Success

What changes can I implement to make life easier?

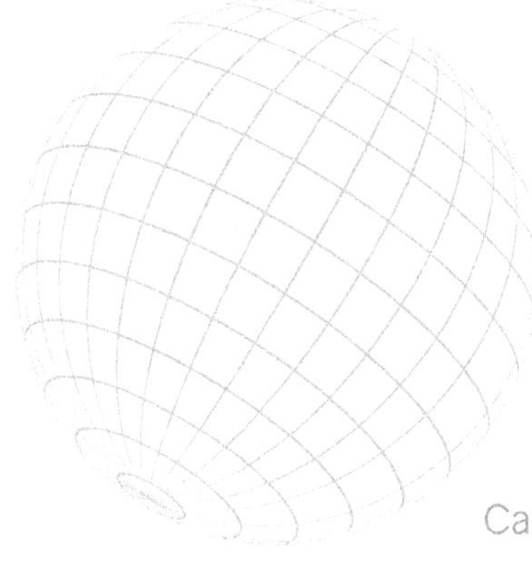

My Support System

People and organizations I can call for support:

My Support System

People and organizations I can call for support:

My Support System

People and organizations I can call for support:

My Support System

People and organizations I can call for support:

Self-Care Routine

Self-Care Routine

Caregiver's Self-Care Notebook

Self-Care Goals

Self-Care Goals

Self-Care Goals

Expressions of Gratitude

My Health & Wellness Management

My Health & Wellness Management

Caregiver's Self-Care Notebook

My Health & Wellness Management

My Health & Wellness Management

Caregiver's Self-Care Notebook

My Health & Wellness Management

Caregiver's Self-Care Notebook

Notes

Notes

Notes

Notes

Notes

Notes

Caregiver's Self-Care Notebook

Notes

Notes

Caregiver's Self-Care Notebook